# THE
# DECISION
# IS IN YOUR
# HAND

Kenneth W. Gilmore, Sr.

Copyright © 2002 by Kenneth W. Gilmore Sr.

*The Decision Is in Your Hand*
by Kenneth W. Gilmore Sr.

Printed in the United States of America
ISBN 09729275-2-2

Unless otherwise quoted, all Scripture quotations are from the Holy Bible, New King James Version. Copyright © 1982 Thomas Nelson, Inc.

Scripture quotations marked KJV are from the King James Version of the Bible

Scripture quotations marked NIV are from the Holy Bible, New International Version. Copyright © 1973, 1978, 1984, International Bible Society.

Scripture quotations marked NLT are from the Holy Bible, New Living Translation. Copyright © 1996 by Tyndale House Publishers, Inc., Wheaton, IL 60189.

Scripture quotations marked NASB are taken from the NEW AMERICAN STANDARD BIBLE?®, Copyright © 1960, 1962, 1963, 1971, 1972, 1973, 1975, 1977, 1995 by The Lockman Foundation. Used by permission.

Published by Kenneth W. Gilmore, Sr. Ministries

# PREFACE

This book came about as a result of almost two years of writing a weekly bulletin article for the Vaughn Street Church of Christ where I served as Associate Minister with Dewayne Winrow.

I have received many responses to the quality and inspiration of the articles and the encouragement they have brought to many. Therefore, I decided to put these articles into book form to provide a tool for inspiration and devotion to a much wider audience. Many of the articles came out of my own personal experience, some of which were quite painful.

These ideas represent "decision passages" that I entered beginning in the fall of 1993 after my life had come to a screeching halt as a result of a very painful divorce.

This was a time of major transition, a time of doubt, dismay and discouragement. I went through a period were I felt like "damaged goods" with no real opportunity to serve in full-time ministry to continue to use the gifts God had blessed me with. I can say that God comforts His children through times of pain and disillusionment, and ultimately out of the depths of that pain. He gives a new vision of a brighter tomorrow.

# DEDICATION

I am proud to dedicate this book to my family. To my mother, Ollie Gilmore, who has left us to be with the Lord. She taught me to believe in myself and in God. To my siblings: Oliver, Eddie, Gloria, Betty, Virginia, Lamar, Margie, Vickie, and Darryl. To my son, Kenneth Jr., who serves as a constant joy and inspiration to me. Without my family's support, memories, help, encouragement and prayers this book would not have been possible.

# ACKNOWLEDGMENTS

It is impossible to write a book like this one without the help of "foundational-level" people.

*Special thanks to:*
Dewayne Winrow and the Vaughn Street Church family for giving me a second chance in the ministry.

Earlene Bryson, the church secretary, who originally typed many of these articles for the weekly bulletin. Thank you for your friendship and the many conversations and tears of pain and joy we experienced together.

To Marty, a very close and personal friend, who taught me the art of friendship and love.

To Dr. Andrew J. Hairston, a mentor and a personal friend who has shaped my life beyond his teaching.

To Frank McKinney, who supported me financially while a student at Pepperdine University. Thank you so much for believing in me.

This book is sent forward with great excitement to be an inspiration to individuals struggling with a personal crisis or looking for direction to begin again. This book is intended to help you never stop believing in yourself and in God. The decision to move on is in your hand!

# TABLE OF CONTENTS

THE DECISION IS IN YOUR HAND

THE DECISION IS IN YOUR HAND

# J INTRODUCTION

July 1992, February 1993 and September 1993, are three pivotal months indelibly etched in my mind. Their importance cannot be understated because they have radically transformed me.

- July 1992 was when my father died.
- February 1993 was when my mother departed to be with the Lord. She was truly a committed believer.

- September 1993 was the beginning of the very painful break-up of my marriage.

These back-to-back events over the course of fourteen months changed the direction of my life. This book is the story of my decision to begin again in spite of a pending divorce and the loss of employment opportunities to serve congregations of the Churches of Christ.

I was "damaged goods" and so my life went through a series of turns. To begin the process of rebuilding my life I moved from Tampa, Florida to Dallas, Texas. It was time to put some perspective on all that had transpired.

This was extremely difficult, because reality dictated that I no longer would have a wife and would have to leave my one-year-old son, Kenneth Jr., behind. The haunting question in the back of my mind was, "Would he remember me?"

I had no job, no car, and only three hundred dollars to my name when I boarded a Greyhound bus bound for Dallas. All the while I hoped that something would happen to awaken me from this nightmare and that my wife would suddenly appear pleading for me not to leave.

When I arrived in Dallas, my living arrangements with a friend fell through. With nowhere else to turn, I found myself in a Motel 6 on the south side of Dallas. With only a hundred dollars in my pocket, I began to wonder who I might know that could help me through this difficult transition in my life.

I soon learned that a former professor of mine from Abilene Christian University, Dr. Lynn Anderson, was preaching at the Preston Road Church of Christ. Immediately, I called the church office and spoke to the secretary. She informed me that Lynn was out of town and so could not speak to him.

Needing help, I asked to speak with an elder involved in the benevolence program. I told the elder who I was and that I was a former student of Dr. Anderson's. I explained

THE DECISION IS IN YOUR HAND

that I had just relocated to Dallas from Tampa, was separated from my wife pending divorce, had very little money and needed a place to live. The elder told me they could give two hundred and fifty dollars to assist in my housing predicament. Thanking him, I set out to see what God would do.

God works in mysterious ways His wonder to declare. I found an apartment next to Dallas Theological Seminary on Swiss Avenue. I told the apartment manager of my predicament and explained that all the money I had was from the check the Preston Road Church of Christ had just given me.

The manager said she would allow me to move in with two hundred fifty dollars, but would have to pay the rent by the end of the month. I had thirty days to make some money to be able to meet that obligation. With no car, I quickly learned how to get around Dallas on the public transportation system.

Through a young lady name Maria at El

Centro Community College in Dallas, I was able to get a job working as a substitute teacher in the Irving Independent School District. Every morning, I had to rise about 5:30 AM to catch the earliest bus that would carry me from east Dallas to Irving, Texas. During the week I taught as a substitute, but on the weekends was preaching and conducting leadership workshops to pay bills.

So there I was in Dallas, nearly fifteen thousand dollars in debt, living in an apartment with no furniture and sleeping on the floor, cooking with utensils and silverware acquired from the Salvation Army Thrift store and using milk crates as a table.

When I was not out teaching or conducting workshops, I attended the Greenville Avenue Church of Christ. Thanks to God, I was able to do quite a number of workshops in California, Florida, Tennessee, South Carolina and Michigan. While in Michigan doing a leadership workshop, my friend, Cedric Townsend, introduced me to Brother McKenzie King, a godly man who became a great blessing to me. I told him that I was in need of a car and understood that he had one to sell.

I told brother King that I had no money, but would be willing to work out terms that would be acceptable to him. He said, "Brother Gilmore, I'll let you take the car with you, and give you the title. Then, when you've gotten things together in your life, send me what you think you can afford."

Through Brother King, God blessed me with a beautiful, top of the line Buick Park Avenue. I'm telling you, that as I drove that vehicle back to Dallas, I was ridin' high in the Lord.

I decided to return to Florida in April 1994, but this time I would move to Orlando. Only seventy-four miles from Tampa, Orlando was a clean, beautiful and friendly city I had always liked. I missed my son, so my decision to go back to Florida was due in large part to the fact that I still hoped for some kind of reconciliation, though this would never happen.

Paternalistic instinct was the source of my rationale to return to Florida. I had made a promise to myself that, since I didn't grow up with my father, if God ever blessed me with children I would never abandon nor leave them.

I arrived in Orlando in the summer of 1994 and was faced again with meager resources. I rented a small office on Orange Blossom Trail, one of the main strips in Orlando and continued to do workshops, but they were few in number. Because I couldn't afford the deposit and first month's rent for an apartment, I slept in my office.

One day, I had no money and knew no one from whom I could get any. That day, I met Bob Thompson, an older African American gentlemen who had an office next to mine. I said, "Bob, I have no money. I haven't eaten anything all day, and I'm hungry. Will you lend me five dollars?"

Bob said, "Come with me" and he took me to a place called Ryan's Steak House. They had a buffet and you could eat all you wanted, so that night I ate all I could. Bob said, "Ken, I can show you how to make some easy money so you'll never have to worry about food or money again." I was interested in what he had to say because I knew that the next day I'd be in the same predicament. He said, "Tomorrow we'll go to Home Depot, buy some paint and stencils and will put address numbers down."

You may be wondering why I didn't file for unemployment or get on welfare. Believe me, I tried. I was told that the time to file had lapsed from my last job in order to have a valid claim. Furthermore, I didn't have a permanent address.

Thus started my painting career. I painted address numbers on the curbs where people lived, charging each house only five dollars. My goal was to do twenty houses a day, one hundred dollars a day, six hundred dollars a week. I was making more money painting address numbers than what I would have received from welfare or unemployment!

Eventually I was able to get a room in a

hotel. Then I applied for a teaching position with the Orlando Public School System working in an alternative education program with students who were on the verge of being expelled for disciplinary reasons.

During this time, I worked with two African American ladies who became friends and surrogate mothers to me. They encouraged me to go back to school and get my education, and that my son would be all right if I stayed in touch with him and visited him when I could. So, I applied to Pepperdine University to work on a doctorate in education. I knew that if I were ever going to change my life, I would need to continue my education. Pepperdine accepted me with a partial scholarship; I had only one more hurdle to clear – finding a job in California to support myself while I went to school.

That's when God opened another door. The Vaughn Street Church of Christ under the leadership of Dewayne Winrow invited me to apply for a recently created position as Associate Minister. I applied and was offered a thirty-day tryout to see if my gifts and talents would be a match for this congregation of the Lord's people.

It seemed like a match, so I was offered a one-year, twenty thousand dollar contract to assist, teach and preach. To some, this may not seem like a lot of money to live in Southern California, but to me, this was God sent for three reasons:

1. I had never made this much money in full-time Christian ministry.
2. Church ministry was something I believed God had called and equipped me for.
3. I would be able to go to school.

To the leaders of the Vaughn Street Church of Christ, I am deeply grateful.

God is still in the miracle business. He is still working in my life and in your life as well. Problems and setbacks will come, but we must *never give up*. We must always remember that it's not what happens <u>to</u> us that matters, but what happens <u>in</u> us.

# 1

# THE DECISION
# IS IN YOUR HAND

You can't control the outward circumstances in your life, but you can control how you will respond and what your attitude will be. The decision is in you hand!

# THE DECISION IS IN YOUR HAND

The story is told of a very wise old man that lived in a small rural village. There was no problem or dilemma that he could not solve. One day a little boy in that village decided that he would try to out smart this wise old man and demonstrate to the whole village that he was not as wise and smart as the townspeople thought.

The little boy came upon an idea, a master plan that would surely get the old wise man. He decided to catch a little bird, go to the old wise man and tell him that there was a little bird in his hand. Then he would ask if the bird was alive or dead. His reasoning was this:

*If the old wise man says that the bird is alive, I will crush the bird in my hand. However, if the old man says the bird is dead, I will open my hand and let the bird go free.*

Putting the plan in action, the little boy asked the old wise man which was true: "Is the bird alive or dead?"

The old wise man said, *"Son, if I say to you that the bird is dead, you will open your hand and let the bird go free. If I say the bird is alive you will crush it in your hand to kill it."* Then the old man startled the boy saying, *"Son, the decision is in your hand – the power of life or death."*

God instructed Israel to choose life and not death in Deuteronomy 30:15-20. If Israel were willing to love God, serve Him and keep His statutes they would have long life and blessings. However, if Israel chose to disobey God, they would experience disease, destruction and death. Therefore, God admonished them to "choose life."

Just as God warned the Israelites to choose life or choose death, so He warns you – the decision is in your hand. You can choose to take charge of your life and live as God would have you live, or you can choose death. When you choose destructive mates or choose to associate with people who have no God conscience, you choose death. Furthermore, you have no one to blame but yourself.

Likewise, you can choose to remain in your current economic plight. You can choose where you live and how you live, that decision is always yours.

You can also decide to play "victim" or rise to be "victorious" and be a champion for God. It's not easy, because there are always those who seek to steal your dream and tell you that you're a nobody with too many obstacles and too much baggage.

Never let others define who you are,

what you are or what you can become. Like it or not, you hold your future. Solomon declared in Proverbs 23:7, *"For as he thinks in his heart, so is he"* (NKJV).

All your life revolves on what you think, most of all on what you think of God. The decision is in your hand whether to stay with your past or to launch out into the deep of your future!

## The Decision To Move On

There comes a time in everyone's life when the moment of decision arrives. We've known for years, months, weeks or days that down in the very core of our soul a drastic change is needed.

There are many stages to our journey of maturity and wholeness. We may experience:

- Pain and loneliness.
- Failure through loss of employment, loss of a relationship or just feeling that our life is stuck and the world is passing us by.

- Pain from having lost our way.
- Loss of focus and direction in life.

The children of Israel had been circling the mountain wandering for some forty years waiting, looking and expecting some sense of direction from God. Finally, the time came when God told Israel's leaders that it was time to move out. A time to move forward had come.

Likewise, the time will come when you must stop feeling sorry for yourself and take responsibility for your life. If you allow broken relationships and unfulfilled promises to abort your journey to fulfillment and joy, you have failed miserably.

Paul declared in 1 Corinthians 10 that Israel should be an example to us, not to rely upon our own human frailty of thought, but to look to our Master and Savior. Take courage from the story of the Prodigal Son who realized he had made a terrible mistake when he had sunk to the lowest point of his life (Luke 15:11-32).

Luke declared that the young man "came to himself" and realized that the moment of truth had come. It was time to decide and to act, not to procrastinate. He knew that he had to take full advantage of every moment that God had given him. Likewise, Paul says you too must redeem the time.

*What will you do?*
*No decision is a decision.*
*God is waiting for you and your*
*future is waiting for you.*
*What are you waiting for?*

## New Directions

Maya Angelou, the famous black poetess, wrote in her 1993 best selling book, <u>Wouldn't Take Nothing For My Journey Now</u> about a lady named Mrs. Annie Johnson. Mrs. Johnson lived in Arkansas and was raising two toddling sons. She had very little money, a slight ability to read and was able to add simple numbers. Add to this picture a disastrous marriage and the burdensome fact that Mrs. Johnson was a big-boned Negro woman over six feet tall.

When Mrs. Johnson's marriage ended, she decided that she would not go to work as a domestic and leave her "precious babes" to anyone else's care. There was no possibility of being hired at the town's cotton gin or lumber mill, but maybe there was a way to make two factories work for her.

In her words, *"I looked up the road I was going and back the way I came, and since I wasn't satisfied, I decided to step off the road and cut me a new path."* Mrs. Johnson noticed that the men who worked in the cotton gin and the lumber mill could use a good hot lunch. She knew she wasn't a fancy cook but also knew that she could *"mix groceries well enough to scare hunger away from a starving man."*

Therefore, Mrs. Johnson set out meticulously, and in secret, to developing her plan of action. Just before lunch, Mrs. Johnson set up in an empty lot behind the cotton gin. As the dinner noon bell rang, she dropped the savors into boiling fat and the aroma rose and floated over the workers who spilled out of the gin.

Business was slow those first days, but Annie was determined. For the next few years, she never disappointed her customers. She had stepped from the road, which seemed to have been chosen for her, and cut herself a brand-new path.

In later years, that stall become a store where customers could buy cheese, meal, syrup, cookies, candy, writing tablets, pickles, canned goods, fresh fruit, soft drinks, coal, oil and leather soles for worn-out shoes.

## The Road Ahead

We have the right and the responsibility to assess the roads that lie ahead and those over which we have traveled. If the future road looms ominous or unpromising and the roads back uninviting, then we need to gather our resolve and, carrying only the necessary baggage, step off that road into another direction. If the new choice is also unpalatable, then we must be ready to change that as well, without embarrassment.

The New Testament calls this new direction "repentance" – a change of mind that results in a change of action. It's a decision to move in the direction of God's plan and will for your life. Do you need to step off the road you are currently traveling? If so, in what new direction do you need to go?

Bill Gates, the billionaire genius and founder of Microsoft Corporation, has written a popular best selling book entitled, **The Road Ahead**. Gates forecasts the vast changes that are coming in the $21^{st}$ Century, discussing such topics as:

- What is the Information Super-Highway?
- How will technology change our lives?
- Does one have to learn how to use a computer?
- Will your job become obsolete?

Furthermore, Gates says that technology will forever change the way we buy, work, learn, and communicate with each other.

This visionary leader is setting out before our very eyes the "stuff" that will shape and mold us whether we like it or not. That is scary and yet very powerful.

Solomon declared, *"Where there is no vision, the people are unrestrained"* (Prov 29:18 NASB).

Therefore, some answers you must seek include:

- What do you see ahead for your life?
- How is God shaping your life for the future?
- How will the church look further down the road?
- What profound changes will occur that affect how congregations do ministry?

It's my prayer that you will become more sensitive to the leading of God's Spirit. That in your heart you'll pray, *"Lord I don't know what the future holds, but I know who holds the future."*

I look forward with great anticipation to what really and truly lies ahead. It's mind blowing what the Lord can do with people who will humble themselves before Him. Let's be admonished by the words of Jude, *"Earnestly contend for the faith"* (Jude 1:3).

What will you do? Will you press on to pursue God's will or will you be defeated by criticism, hate and lies?

I say to you, PRESS ON!

## The Best Is Yet to Come

Many people are nostalgic about the past and speak fondly of the "good old days." They yearn for the simpler things of life because times are so complicated. Nostalgia threatens their future because they are living in the past and comparing it to the future.

However, we must embrace the future with its new possibilities and new challenges all the while avoiding the mistakes of the past. Greater opportunities afford the privilege of fulfilling our destiny as the people of God.

When we prepare ourselves to be insightful about our world, we can capitalize on opportunities that may bring us not only personal success and achievement, but recognition to the God of heaven as well. God has placed us strategically in our various occupations so that His name will be manifested to those persons who don't have a personal relationship with Him.

Yes. The future is uncertain, but it's filled with new possibilities to maximize your ability through Christ. Paul declared, *"I can do all things through Him who strengthens me"* (Phil 4:13). The Best is Yet To Come!!!

## Moving Forward

The children of Israel were in Egyptian bondage for four centuries. Finally, after their cries had reached the ear of the Lord and after a series of divine plagues sent on

Egypt, Pharaoh was convinced to release the people of God. Their deliverance came through the leadership of Moses, ending their long years of pain and humiliation.

Exodus 14:1-29 records how after leaving Egypt, Israel was standing on the shores of the Red Sea, ready to move forward to the new land God has promised them. However, Pharaoh's army was pursuing them closing in fast in a last ditch effort to re-capture them. The people of God were afraid, trapped by mountains on both sides, Pharaoh's army pressing their back and the Red Sea in front. What a terrible predicament to be in!

Out of fear and desperation, the people began complaining to Moses. However, Moses told them to be silent and see the salvation of the Lord. Then God instructed him to tell the people to move forward.

*Then they said to Moses, 'Is it because there were no graves in Egypt that you have taken us away to die in the wilderness?' But Moses said to the people, "Do not fear! Stand by and see the salvation of the LORD which He will accomplish for you today; for the Egyptians whom you have seen today, you will never see them again forever. The LORD will fight for you while you keep silent." Then the LORD said to Moses, "Why are you crying out to Me? Tell the sons of Israel to go forward."*

(Ex 14:11, 13-15 NASB)

When we're in a dilemma, our tendency is to either freeze in place or look back to see how it was before. The past tends to become comfortable because we are familiar with it and we don't know what the future holds.

Moving forward means that we don't glorify the past and instead recognize the lessons we needed to learn. Besides, if we're really being honest with ourselves, the past wasn't all that great.

We must trust God and move forward into uncharted waters. Imagine Israel's astonishment at seeing the Red Sea part. Imagine their anxiety and fear of being covered by the sea and drowned. However, if they hadn't moved, the army would have overtaken and killed them.

If you don't move forward from your captivity, you will be overcome or drowned. What problems are causing you to stand still rather than move forward?

Don't stop. Keep moving forward. There is a great future for God's people with His protection and guidance. Moving forward shows your trust in God for the outcome of your life. No person, no issue, no circumstance should ever hold you bondage. Move Forward!

## Picking Up the Pieces of A Broken Dream

Some people have never realized their dreams or ambitions and have found life to be filled with disappointments. They've been ambushed by the circumstances of life and their hearts are wrenched and broken. They discover that they were never prepared to handle the unforeseen or unpredictable and are not as prepared or confident as they once were.

Questions haunt their existence like...

- How should I respond to the uncertainties, the ambiguity, and the absurdity of life?

- How should I make sense of the pain my heart is experiencing because of some traumatic or unsettling event(s)?

Jesus knows that this kind of brokenness and hollowness is pervasive to the human situation. The Master left us these words in John 14:1 *"Let not your hearts be troubled."* Don't be traumatized, shaken or disturbed while agonizing over the separation and isolation that life brings, whether through:

- Death
- Divorce
- Separation

- Feeling that you have no support system
- No one to talk with
- Being alone
- Feeling that your life doesn't count

Many men and women have died with a broken heart. Circumstances may have gotten to the point where they could endure the duress no longer. Successful is the person who **believes in God** and who trusts God for the outcome of their life.

Recognize that God is sovereign, that He rules and that He is Lord. Having a strong faith and confidence in the One who sustains, protects, and provides for us is the key to overcoming <u>any</u> of life's setbacks and the stinging arrows of criticism. Paul wrote in Philippians 4:6-7:

*Be anxious for nothing, but in everything by prayer and supplication with thanksgiving. Let your requests be made known to God. And the peace of God, which surpasses all understand-*

*ing, will guard your hearts and minds through Christ Jesus.*

You <u>can</u> pick up the pieces of a broken heart. God will mend your heart and will touch you like no one else can. He will comfort and sustain you and will show you that there is a brighter tomorrow beyond your present pain and discomfort.

"'*For I know the plans that I have for you,*' *declares the LORD,* '*plans for welfare and not for calamity to give you a future and a hope*'" (Jer 29:11 NASB).

Therefore, TRUST GOD!!!

## The On-Purpose Person

My dear friend, Kevin McCarthy, wrote an interesting little book entitled, <u>The On-Purpose Person</u>. Kevin's objective is to help people make sense of their lives by having a definite purpose and plan and then living each moment with that purpose in mind.

Life is a progressive journey and how one chooses what is important will dictate what their life will become. Many people have good intentions, but they have no action plan to guide and direct their steps.

A journey requires advance preparation, an itinerary, travel accessories and a list of friends to see along the way. The fastest way to achieve your goal and purpose in life is to stay the course.

Jeremiah declared, *"I know, O LORD, that a man's life is not his own; it is not for man to direct his steps"* (Jer 10:23 NIV). Every day of our Christian journey, we need the Lord to guide us through the minefields of life. The apostle Paul said that the devil throws his fiery darts to destroy us in our purpose to reach heaven (Eph 6:16).

Jesus is our model and example for living. He lived with the single-minded purpose of always pleasing His Father. Jesus constantly stayed in touch with the Father to receive direction for the next phase of His grueling ministry.

We must never drift in our purpose to serve God. When we do, we see the effects of a life that is not under the Lordship of Jesus Christ. Paul clearly spelled out how Jesus knew who He was, where He was going, and what His divine mission was all about (Phil. 2:1-5).

Jesus was not interested in debating His mission. He took action and began to prepare the followers who would take up the mantle of leadership once He left to go back to heaven.

Are you on purpose today in your life? Are you on-purpose with God? ...your children? ...your spouse? If not, then today, at this moment, become an On-Purpose Person.

CHAPTER TWO

# LIVING WITH A DIVINE PURPOSE

# Living With A Divine Purpose

These words of Dr. Martin Luther King, Jr. demonstrate that he understood the eternal sacrifice that one must make for what he believes, even if that sacrifice means death.

*"If a man doesn't have a cause to die for, he is not fit to live, and if he sells himself short, even though his body may be young, he is dead, even though the breath and the motions of life go on and on."*

We live in a time when people hold on to very little. Their lives are shaped only by their economic interests and not by any moral or ethical values. We live in a ruthless society driven by the credo of looking out for #1.

The book of Daniel contains a story about four young men that had made up their minds to live with a divine purpose that would shape their words, their thoughts and their deeds.

They were offered the finest of food and drink, and the best education that money could buy if they were loyal and faithful to the king. However, these four young men knew there was a high price to pay and they were unwilling to pay it.

The Bible says that Daniel made up his mind not to defile himself with the king's choicest foods (Dan 1:19). Daniel knew that any encroachment on his faith, no matter how insignificant it might seem, would open the floodgates of compromise in his faith in God. Furthermore, Daniel knew that he must hold the line because God had a special purpose for his life. Daniel knew that God was counting on him to be His representative though he was in exile.

We often make excuses as to why we cannot live out our faith effectively. Have we not etched in our hearts the commitment to live our lives with a divine purpose? Will we glorify God in our words, thoughts and deeds?

Only when we make a stand for God can we see the subtle encroachments on our faith in which Satan seeks to find a foothold. Examine your life. Are you living with a divine purpose and direction for your life?

All eternity is waiting anxiously to see the sons of God come into their glory (Rom 8:19). They will do so because they've lived as God has appointed for the time He has allotted them in this world.

## Is God for Us?

The question of God's loyalty to us often comes to mind when faced with disappointment. Jesus asked this question in a differ-

THE DECISION IS IN YOUR HAND

ent way when He was crucified by quoting Psalm 22:1: *"My God, My God, why hast Thou forsaken me?"*

This question is one of pain, utter loneliness and the feeling that part of your life is slipping away. As you continue to live, the certainty of problems is ever present. The key is to remember that God is with you, in you and for you. Continue to trust Him; He'll not let you down.

The greatest consolation that you can have as a believer is the assurance that you are under God's watchful eye. God's promise is that in the midst of the storm He stands with you.

Mark 4:35-41 tells about a storm that blew into the disciples' life while they were crossing the Sea of Galilee in a ship. Jesus was in the stern of the ship asleep on a cushion when the disciples awakened Him, saying, *"Teacher, do You not care that we are perishing?"*

Jesus arose, rebuked the winds and said to the sea, *"Peace, be still!"* Immediately the wind ceased and there was a great calm. Jesus then turned to the disciples and said, *"Why are you so fearful? How is it that you have no faith?"*

When Jesus is on board in your life, though it may seem He's not there when the storms are present, just have faith and trust Him. Don't be overcome with fear. The Lord cares if you are perishing. When you develop the faith that you're going to trust God, then God will stand in the very midst of your life and calm the storms.

Paul said in Romans 8:32, *"If God is for us, who can be against us."* To have the assurance that we are under divine protection, that we have divine provisions and that we live with a divine purpose, is the greatest secret to walking through whatever storms that may rage in life. As the country and western song says, *"You can walk away a winner"* because God is for us!

## Men for Whom the World Is Not Worthy

Someone once said that history is the life stories of great men who have shaped the eras to their purposes. Men (humankind) have contributed to the advancement of civilization since the dawn of time. Every field of endeavor, arts and sciences, business and education, entertainment and sports are all are testaments to the civility of mankind.

Hebrews 11 dramatically portrays many great men and women of God who endured hardship and persecution but never compromised their integrity and commitment to God. The writer says they experienced hardships, famine, peril, persecution and even death for what they believed. Yet these men and women stand out because they trusted God, even when they had nothing to hold on to but their faith that God would make good on His promises.

Every leader knows that the key to leading a great people is the ability to secure from the people the commitment and ultimate belief that they are on a divine mission.

The story of these great heroes is captured in a parenthetical statement that illustrates their faith, sacrifice and commitment, *"the world was not worthy of them"* (Heb 11:38).

## People With a Purpose

Poet and philosopher Victor Hugo once said, *"Nothing is more powerful than an idea whose time has come."* The time comes in every person's life to rise to the challenge to which each generation is called.

Likewise, God calls each of us to dream for Him and to believe in a cause that is compelling and far greater than we are. We should be moving forward to greatness, not because of what we may possess, but what we might become through God's Spirit living in us.

Peter declared that we *"...are a chosen race, a royal priesthood, a holy nation, a people for God's own possession, that you may proclaim the excellencies of Him who has called you out of darkness into His marvelous light."* (1 Peter 2:9 NASB).

What dreams do you have that are waiting to be born? What visions do you have that will make the world a better place in which to live? The world needs men and women who are not carbon copies, but the real thing.

Be a person who lives with the passion of purpose! God is waiting for you to utilize the gifts and talents that He has blessed you with.

## See It, Say It, Seize It

Some people are eternal pessimists. No matter what the view, all they see is bad. Progress is never determined without struggle, and incremental steps along the way determine whether complete victory will be achieved.

It has been rightly said that your attitude, not your aptitude, determines your altitude. If you are ever going to change your condition in life, you must change the way you think and see yourself. Paul admonished the church at Philippi to focus on four key ideas (Phil 4:1-20):

1. Have the peace of God that surpasses all understanding.
2. Think on those things that are positive and good.
3. In Christ we can accomplish whatever we set our minds to through His power and strength made available to us.
4. Know without a doubt that God will supply all our needs.

Therefore, whatever your dreams or ambitions are that seek to bring glory to God, you must first see it and recognize the possibilities. Declare it. Speak your desires into existence and seize the moment. Take hold of the opportunity, it may never come your way again. See it, say it and seize it!

## Serving the Purpose of God

The Apostle Paul's sermon in the synagogue at Pisidian Antioch told a brief history of Israel and how God raised up men to lead His people (Acts 13:14-41). Paul makes a descriptive statement in that sermon about the life of David, *"For David, after he had served the purpose of God in his own generation, fell asleep, and was laid among his fathers, and underwent decay"* (vs. 36).

Every biblical character that responded to God's call was challenged to live out the purpose of God in his or her life. However, when the "call" came many did not at first choose to seek God's will:

- Moses did not first seek God's purpose to go to Egypt.
- Queen Esther of Persia, did not first seek to pursue God's will for the preservation of the Jewish nation.
- Gideon did not first seek God's purpose to go fight against the Midianites until God showed him a sign.

In contrast, we see early on in the life of David his high commitment and resolve to defend the name of God when the giant Goliath ridiculed the Israelites. This was no novel experience for David because he had previously witnessed the power of God when he defended his flock from both a bear and a lion.

David was described in Scripture as a "man after God's own heart." David reigned as king of Israel for 38 years and established this Jewish nation as a kingdom to be reckoned with. Along the way, he nearly possessed all the land that God had promised to give to the people after leading them out of Egypt centuries earlier.

David had a burning desire to build a temple for God to dwell among His people. He was a passionate man who displayed his love for God in the songs and poetry recorded in the Psalms. These timeless Scriptures have provided comfort for many across the centuries in their refrains of pain, love and loneliness.

It can truthfully be said that David lived out the purpose of God on his life. Are you living your life after the purpose of God? Seek God's purpose for your life, and when the time has come for you to fall asleep and laid to rest, it can be truthfully said that you served the purpose of God in your generation as well!

CHAPTER THREE

# ATTITUDE: THE KEY TO SUCCESS

# ATTITUDE: THE KEY TO SUCCESS

I am convinced that broken relationships and the mismanagement of our lives are directly related to the inability to prioritize the persons, needs and wants in our lives. Knowing that, it's easier to understand the principle of the tithe and why God wants the best and the "first" of who we are and what we possess.

God wants you to first commit yourself to Him. When you do, God knows where your commitments and allegiances really are. Making God first in your life means you will seek His guidance and direction for the decisions regarding your family, career, finances and even your faith.

Consider the "first things" that God requires of us:

- Seek <u>first</u> the Kingdom of God and His righteousness (Matthew 6:33).
- Upon the <u>first</u> day of the week the disciples came together (Acts 20:7).
- They <u>first</u> gave themselves (2 Corinthians 8:5).
- God requires the <u>first</u> fruit of our possession (Proverbs 3:9).
- Upon the <u>first</u> day of the week let everyone of you lay by him in store (1 Corinthians 6:2).
- For if there be <u>first</u> a willing mind (2.Corinthians 8:12).

In light of these scriptural references, are "First" things "first" in your life? Is it possible that you are not experiencing God's blessing because you have not put Him first in everything?

Someone has said that it is not your aptitude (how smart you are), but your attitude that determines your altitude (how high you will fly). How you view yourself largely depends upon how you see God using you to accomplish His will.

## He Died Climbing

Paul wrote in Philippians 4:13, *"I can do all things through Him who strengthens me."* The question is, do you believe it? Take hold of that promise and receive the success and victories that God will bring about in your life.

Jesus is the perfect example of the kind of attitude that we should have. Paul admonished us to have the mind of Christ (Phil 2:1-7) because He always knew who He was in relationship to the Father.

Jesus knew His position and power, therefore it was no problem for Him to become a slave and thus obedient even to the point of death. When you have this kind of disposition, then God will exalt you in due time as He did Christ.

What kind of attitude do you possess? Is it one of arrogance or one of pride? God needs people who can humble themselves and call on His name. Through them, through you, He will accomplish great things.

There is a story of a well-known Swiss mountain climber who was the best in leading expeditions up some of the tallest mountains in the world. One day as he was climbing he was caught in an avalanche. Tragically he was buried and died in the snow. To honor the great achievements of this man who lead expeditions into the splendid beauty of God's creation, his friends and fellow co-workers built a monument at the base of the mountain where he died. It simply read, "He Died Climbing."

What are you climbing toward in this life that will bring you into view of the majesty of God's creation? How many people are you leading by your faith and influence to come to know the Lord? I like the song that says:

*Lord, lift me up and let me stand by faith on heaven's table land, a higher plane than I have found, Lord plant my feet on higher ground. I want to scale the utmost height and catch a gleam of glory bright, though Satan's darts at me are hurled, but still I am pressing on.*

As you continue to climb your mountains for God, there will be steep paths to navigate and many rocks in your way. The key to climbing, as any skillful climber will tell you, is in the shoes you wear and the equipment you carry; you must travel light.

Often while climbing our mountains, people will tell you that you'll never reach the top. The summit of your goals for your family, your education or your commitment to the Lord is out of reach they say. You must not listen to their advice. Instead, focus on the climb because you Just ask the Lord to make your feet like those of a mountain sheep to climb the mountain. If you failed to reach the summit of your life for God or if an avalanche has swept through your life, let it be known that we will only reach the summit step-by-step. It will not be swift and easy; it will be long and hard, but it will be worth the climb.

The writer of Hebrews said, concerning the faith of the Patriarchs, that all of them died in faith, not yet seeing the promise that God promised them (chapter 11). They died while climbing the summit of life for God. Will you die climbing.

## Improving Your Serve

The hours leading up to Jesus' crucifixion were filled with great anxiety. The road leading to the cross was all uphill and a very steep, difficult climb.

John tells the story of Jesus and His disciples during their last meal together before Jesus was delivered up to the Jews. During the supper, Jesus told these rugged

Galileans that one of them would soon betray Him.

Jesus understands the strengths and the weaknesses of fallen humanity. Furthermore, because Jesus knew His source of origin, He knew His ultimate destiny. With this perspective, it's easier to stay focused on the mission.

Jesus was also able to serve others. Jesus was the King of heaven and Creator of all, but with no shame or embarrassment, Jesus wrapped a towel around His waist and washed the disciples' feet. Jesus' attitude was one of servitude. Jesus didn't come to be served, He came to serve. Paul said it best in a letter to the church in Philippi:

*Have this attitude in yourselves which was also in Christ Jesus, who, although He existed in the form of God, did not regard equality with God a thing to be grasped, but emptied Himself, taking the form of a bond-servant, and being made in the likeness of men. And being found in appearance as a man,*

*He humbled Himself by becoming obedient to the point of death, even death on a cross.*

(Phil 2:5-8 NASB)

You, too, can improve your service to others by simply keeping your attitude in check. You do this by serving God and not man. What I mean is that as you are in service to God, you are naturally serving what He values most, other people.

Improve your service to God by getting involved in the life of the church. There are people who need your love and mentoring, there are children who need your tutoring. Youth everywhere need volunteers to share their wisdom and experience to prepare our young people for the future.

Jesus taught that the greatest among you would be your servant. Do you seek to be great? Then improve your serve!

## How to Define Greatness

People define greatness and success using many criterion, including:

- Financial status
- Freedom to do what they love to do
- Making a significant contribution to mankind
- Finding a lifetime companion

The Bible teaches that success in God's eyes is not determined by these factors no matter how important they are. What determines a person's real greatness is their love for God.

When you fully comprehend God's love for you, you will appreciate the source of true happiness. Jesus said in Matthew 16:26, *"For what will a man be profited, if he gains the whole world, and forfeits his soul? Or what will a man give in exchange for his soul?"*

God's desire for His people has always been for them to be great and thus demonstrate His love to the world. We can never change the world or ourselves until God is at the center of our lives. He must change us first.

Daniel of old said that when we surrender to God, we as *"people who know their God shall be strong, and carry out great exploits"* (Daniel 11:32).

Do you desire greatness? Do you want to make a lasting contribution? Then carry out great exploits by helping change the world for Jesus Christ!

## The Greatness of Giving

For many, the idea of greatness is far-fetched. *"How could I ever do great exploits for God?"* they wonder. However, the pathway to greatness is paved with service to others. What enables one to serve is the sense that they've been served.

We love because we are loved. Therefore, serving others springs out of an inward attitude of thankfulness for what God has done for us. By investing in the lives of others, we lay up treasure in Heaven that is immune to earthly market conditions and recession.

Giving thanks for what God has done is illustrated every year during the holidays. Volunteerism usually reaches its peak around Thanksgiving and Christmas. This time of the year is a time of sharing, giving thanks and of remembrance.

The Lord has blessed us in ways that have not yet been fully realized. The wisdom of King Solomon is well express in Ecclesiastes, where he paints a vivid picture of the proper balance necessary in our lives:

*There is a time for everything,*

*and a season for every activity under*

> *heaven:*

*a time to be born and a time to die,*

*a time to plant and a time to uproot,*

*a time to kill and a time to heal,*

*a time to tear down and a time to build,*

*a time to weep and a time to laugh,*

*a time to mourn and a time to dance,*

*a time to scatter stones and a time to*

> *gather them,*

*a time to embrace and a time to refrain,*

*a time to search and a time to give up,*

*a time to keep and a time to throw*

> *away,*

*a time to tear and a time to mend,*

*a time to be silent and a time to speak,*

*a time to love and a time to hate,*

*a time for war and a time for peace.*

*What does the worker gain from his toil? I have seen the burden God has laid on men. He has made everything beautiful in its time. He has also set eternity in the hearts of men; yet they cannot fathom what God has done from beginning to end. I know that there is nothing better for men than to be happy and do good while they live.*

*(Eccl 3:1-12 NIV)*

There are times to remember what God has done for you, and a time to remember what others have contributed to the quality of your life. There is a time to give thanks for blessings and gifts received. Therefore, give thanks for the opportunities that have been afforded you, for out of these blessings you will share your joy, your laughter and your pain.

Be thankful for the blessings that God has shown through the generosity of others in their kindness toward you. Likewise, never forget those who are less fortunate and try to be a blessing to them in some way as well. The spirit of giving thanks is contagious when you remember that God gave His only Son.

## Things Are Not Always As they Seem

When you study the lives of great Biblical characters, you see their faith and how they responded to God's call to ministry. Let's briefly examine the lives of Joseph, Moses and Joshua to see how God prepared them to be leaders of Israel.

### Joseph

Joseph served as a slave in Potiphar's house and servant in the jailer's quarters.

During those times of trial, it may not have seemed to Joseph that the dreams he had as a young boy were going as they should. Nevertheless, Joseph stayed true to God, saying:

> Then Joseph said to his brothers, "Come close to me." When they had done so, he said, "I am your brother Joseph, the one you sold into Egypt! And now, do not be distressed and do not be angry with yourselves for selling me here, because it was to save lives that God sent me ahead of you. For two years now there has been famine in the land, and for the next five years there will not be plowing and reaping. But God sent me ahead of you to preserve for you a remnant on earth and to save your lives by a great deliverance. "So then, it was not you who sent me here, but God."
>
> (Gen 45:4-8 NIV)

## Moses

Moses was raised in the house of Pharaoh after being discovered floating in a basked on the Nile. Because of his high estate, Moses was privileged and was in line to assume the throne. However, after seeing the plight of his Hebrew kinsmen, he sought to take matters into his own hand and killed an Egyptian who was mistreating one of the Jews. Fear gripped Moses and he fled for his life. Because of this experience, Moses, at the age of forty, was convinced that he could not be an effective leader much less an emancipator.

Nevertheless, God called Moses at the ripe old age of eighty. Youth and zeal wouldn't be enough to deliver God's people. It would take God's strength in an eighty-year-old Moses, not human strength in a forty-year-old Moses. So when God called, Moses knew that if he were to deliver God's people, it wouldn't be by his own strength, but by God's strength.

### Joshua

Joshua paid the price as well. He spent forty years in preparation to become Israel's leader after Moses and to distribute the Promised Land to the people. His preparation began in earnest when he stood against Amalek while Aaron and Hur held up Moses' arms.

The battle swung to and fro, back and forth. First, Israel would prevail then the Amalekites would surge ahead. Though the battle may not have gone as Joshua desired, it was won because God was fighting the war.

The same is true with us. When it seems that things are not turning out as we had planned and hoped, God is still working behind the scenes accomplishing His divine will. Romans 8:28 declares: *"And we know that God causes all things to work together for good to those who love God, to those who are called according to His purpose"* (NASB).

Joseph, Moses and Joshua had to trust God, because often what they saw made no sense in the natural realm. Paul declared in 2 Corinthians 5:7 that, "...*we walk by faith and not by sight.*" Again in 2 Corinthians 4:16: "*For we look at things not seen, that are eternal.*"

Things are not always as they seem and God often comes through just when you are about to quit. Don't lose heart and don't faint in the battle. Remember, "*This is what the LORD says to you: 'Do not be afraid or discouraged because of this vast army. For the battle is not yours, but God's'*" (2 Chron 20:15 NIV)

# 4

# HANDLING LIFE'S TEMPTATIONS

# HANDLING LIFE'S TEMPTATIONS

Life is full of ups and downs that seek to abort one's journey to fulfillment and joy. The writer of Hebrews said it well, *"Therefore, since we have so great a cloud of witnesses surrounding us, let us also lay aside every encumbrance, and the sin which so easily entangles us, and let us run with endurance the race that is set before us"* (Heb 12:1 NASB).

I've discovered that Christians who've been successful at minimizing sin in their lives did not haphazardly end up living whole-some, significant lives for the Glory of God. These people, regardless of education or financial stability, have continually and con-sistently made right choices and recognized the dangers of capricious living.

Any decisions you make that are rooted in the flesh reap consequences that may take a lifetime to resolve. The Apostle Paul advises how to handle life's temptations in the midst of a very distorted and twisted society. Satan will bring persons, events and situations into your life designed to make you fall. Paul wrote:

> *Therefore let him who thinks he stands take heed lest he fall. No temp-tation has overtaken you but such as is common to man; and God is faithful, who will not allow you to be tempted beyond what you are able, but with the temptation will provide the way of escape also, that you may be able to endure it.*
>
> (1 Cor 10:12-13 NASB)

## Five Steps to Handling Temptation

*Step #1: Critically evaluate and assess your-self to understand our own weaknesses and frailties.* Satan never presents you with things not desired in your will. Therefore, if you think you're strong, look at the areas of your life most vulnerable to the subtle approaches of Satan.

*Step #2: The temptations you face are common to the rest of the human family.* You can make no excuses about giving in to the desires of the carnal nature and believe that no one else has ever been through what you are going through.

*Step #3: Tap in to the faithfulness of God.* Remember that no matter what you are going through, God is faithful.

*Step #4: Remember that God will not allow you to be tempted beyond what you are able to withstand.* God will see you through the temptation. He knows how much you can bear and how far you can go.

*Step #5: Look for the escape route provided by God.* God always provides an open door of escape. However, you must not become entangled in your trials and mistakes. Focus on how to live on a higher and more positive level, not only for God, but for your own peace of mind as well.

## Are You Running on Empty?

Monumental changes occur at laser speed in today's fast-paced society. Modern technology is found everywhere, in our cars, homes and the workplace. Even fast food restaurants are designed to make our lives easier and less complicated. These changes are for our benefit and are supposed to give us more time to do the things we like doing most.

Many people live in a fantasyland and daydream of better times, better things and better jobs. They live in the land of "If only…" and think things like:

- If only I can make it until I retire, then….
- If only I had enough money, I could pay all of my bills and live life to the fullest.
- If only I could find the house (car, spouse, job, etc.) of my dreams, life would really be worth living.

With all our modern advances as a society, we still don't have much time to do the things we enjoy. We worry about our children, our jobs and whether we'll be laid off. Many things clamor for our attention and crowd our spaces of serenity and peace.

*Do you feel sometimes that you are running on empty? Do you need to have your tank refueled and your batteries recharged?*

Jesus said that *"your Father knows what you need, before you ask Him…do not be* anxious for your life...seek first His kingdom and His righteousness; and all these things shall be added to you" (Matthew 6:8,25,33).

The Apostle Paul exhorted the Galatians to "...not lose heart in doing good, for in due time we shall reap if we do not grow weary" (Galatians 6:9).

Sometimes, busy schedules and over commitments cause us to run ourselves into the ground. Finally, our bodies give out and the rest and relaxation we really need is forced upon us. Often when running on empty, we're living on the fumes of past achievements and the old foggy memories of days gone by. The zest is gone from our lives, we have no pep and the sparkle in our eyes is gone.

When we are tired and sluggish, we are vulnerable to be deceived. It's then that the evil one approaches with subtle deception to tempt us in our vulnerability.

Are you running on empty? Are you living on the glory of past successes, no longer stretching for the goal of the high prize?

Remember, Paul admonished you to run to win and to look unto Jesus, the author and finisher of your faith (1 Cor 9:27).

Take time to refuel and recharge your batteries. Like Jesus, you must value the importance of simple rest and relaxation.

## Check Your Contract

Just as important as recharging and refueling is to the body, so is the need to periodically review and examine your commitments. This enables you to enhance the commitments that are of great value and to drop those that are of little or no worth.

If you've ever received a credit card, you've also received a contract that will explain the terms of your agreement with the bank. You'll know the amount of the line of credit extended, what the interest rate is and what remedies are available to both you and the bank in the event of a breech of contract. Often, accompanying the card and contract will be a letter expressing how happy the bank is that you are a customer.

The purpose of the contract is to help you understand the responsibilities of the privileges that come with the use of the credit card. It clearly expresses the importance of having a commitment to pay according to the terms set forth. This call to commitment can either be in generalized terms or in operational terms that enable you to understand what is being agreed upon.

Another important example is your membership in the local church. Are you a contributing member? Being a contributing member is much more than just giving money, it's being committed to the vision of the house.

Have you ever wondered why some members of the church don't take their membership seriously? When a person becomes a member of the church, they promise to support the church with their prayers, presence, service and gifts.

When you become a member of the

church, you enter into a three-fold psychological contract or covenant...

- between you and God
- you and other believers
- to support the church

In return, the church provides its members opportunities for:

- Corporate worship to demonstrate a ministry of concern, celebrating times of both sadness and joy
- Spiritual growth
- Involvement in ministry
- Personal witness and service
- To treat each member as a person, not as an object

Have you recently checked your psychological and spiritual commitment to God, others and to the church? Are you living up to the pledge and commitment you made? Is your attitude one of apathy or of thanksgiving? Check your contract!

## Leaves From the Notes of a Tamed Cynic

Part of checking the contract is regularly doing a thorough self-examination. Yes. The Holy Spirit works in you to perfect you in Christ, but that doesn't mean you can sit back on your heels and let God do it all. You share some responsibility in your growth and maturity.

Have you ever stopped to pick up a piece of paper because you've noticed an interesting picture, headline or statement on it? Often, you will see something that catches the eye but will later throw it away because it's just trash.

The world in which we live is a fascinating place. We are interested in news about crime, employment, entertainment and education, though much of it is negative and critical of government, private industry, education, or political, social and religious leaders. Hardly ever do we hear exciting news about someone making radical changes in their life for the better.

Eugene Peterson said, *"We are a nation of bored insomniacs; we are spectators to overgrown athletes who have overgrown egos."* As a nation, we are thrilled at chaos and misery and we've become carriers of negative, unhealthy information that brings no good to either the bearer or the one who is the object of the poison.

The Bible declares, *"let everyone be quick to hear, slow to speak and slow to anger"* (James 1:19). Be careful what you say about others. It could ruin a person's integrity and good name that has taken years to build. Be careful that you have all the facts because what you may perceive, though reality in your mind, may not be reality at all.

Don't carry the message of destruction looking for someone to destroy. Paul wrote that we are letters of Christ, written on the heart to be known and read by all men, written not with ink, but with the spirit of the living God (2 Cor 3:1-7 paraphrased).

Don't be a leaf from the notes of a tamed cynic. Don't be one who constantly complains and is negative about everything. Don't bring only negative news, be a positive influence on someone's life. You never know when you'll be a tool in the hand of God to turn a cynical heart toward the Father.

*CHAPTER FIVE*

# CONVINCED, CONVICTED, BUT NOT CONVERTED

# CONVINCED, CONVICTED, BUT NOT CONVERTED

The United States is a very cosmopolitan nation. People from around the globe call this country home and revel in the freedom of expression that we enjoy. However, the very freedoms we have learned to love and to which we've become accustomed allow and even enable many diverse belief systems to be in operation at the same time. No longer are we considered a Christian nation. Instead, we are post-Christian and embrace the ideology that many paths lead to God.

At this time in human history, many belief systems are espoused in varying forms and fashions. What a person believes are the assumptions upon which their life is built and focused. Many people know that they need a change in their lives and believe that they really do need God. Nevertheless, to truly be convicted of the changes needed in their lives, requires total abandonment of the course they are presently on.

Knowing something is more than simply being convinced because the idea or concept is rational or has plausibility. To be convicted means that a person has a vested emotional interest in a concept or issue. True conviction leads one to action based upon a set of beliefs or assumptions.

Many people say that they believe in God, the Bible and the church and yet are never motivated to set in motion the commitment they made in the presence of witnesses. Their life belongs to God because they've been bought with a price (1 Cor 6: 20) but they continue to live as they did before any commitment was made.

Conversion means that you've been regenerated by the power of Christ through the Holy Spirit. Regeneration changes the direction of your life through transformation of the inner man by the Holy Spirit and the principles of Jesus' word. Conversion means that you've released all claims of ownership in your life and have received from God a lifetime lease to live to the greatest fulfillment of His Divine objective.

These questions beg answering as you examine to whom you belong:

- Are you just convinced about God?
- Are you convicted by your own failures and sin?
- Are you truly converted to the principles of God's word?
- Does God reside in your life consistently?
- Do you believe intellectually, but not in living and working out your conversion experience?
- Are you truly converted?

Take Paul's advice today if you aren't sure of where you stand in light of the above questions.

*As God's fellow workers we urge you not to receive God's grace in vain. For he says,*

> *'In the time of my favor I heard you,*
>
>    *and in the day of salvation I helped you.'*

*<u>I tell you, now is the time of God's favor, now is the day of salvation.</u>*

(2 Cor 6:1-2 NIV)

*EPILOGUE*

# HOW TO BE SAVED: FIVE STEPS OF SALVATION

The Bible teaches that man is lost and in need of a Savior. Sin has separated man and God. However, God has made provision to rescue, deliver and restore man back into loving fellowship with Him through His Son, Jesus Christ.

Man must be convicted of his sin, accept the provision of righteousness, which is Jesus Christ, or face eternity without God.

God wants the best for you. He created you to have fellowship with Him and to exercise dominion over the earth (Gen 1:26-27).

To accept God's provision of salvation, you must...

1. **Hear the gospel:** "So then faith comes by hearing, and hearing by the word of God" (Romans 10:17).

2. **Believe in the gospel:** *"Moreover, brethren, I declare to you the gospel which I preached to you, which also you received and in which you stand, by which also you are saved, if you hold fast that word which I preached to you—unless you believed in vain. For I delivered to you first of all that which I also received: that Christ died for our sins according to the Scriptures, and that He was buried, and that He rose again the third day according to the Scriptures"* (1 Cor 15:1-4).

3. **Repent, which means you change your mind resulting in a change of actions and direction:** *"Then Peter*

*said to them, "Repent, and let every one of you be baptized in the name of Jesus Christ for the remission of sins; and you shall receive the gift of the Holy Spirit"* (Acts 2:38). *"I tell you...unless you repent you will...perish"* (Luke 13:3).

4. **Confess your lost state and agree with God to accept His provision, Jesus Christ:** *"Therefore whoever confesses Me before men, him I will also confess before My Father who is in heaven"* (Matt 10:32).

5. **Be baptized for the remission of sin:** *"And now why are you waiting? Arise and be baptized, and wash away your sins, calling on the name of the Lord"* (Acts 22:16).

Locate a Church of Christ in your area with whom to worship.

# OTHER BOOKS BY DR. KENNETH GILMORE

Leadership In African American Churches of Christ

The New Covenant: Your Rights and Privileges

What Is Biblical Faith?

The Battle for the Mind

Bring Me The Book

The Apostle's Doctrine

Money: God's Financial Plan For Your Life

Unmasking Satanic Lies

The Authority of The Believer

Principle Centered Living

The Power of The Tongue

Prayer, The Key To Success

God's Spiritual Laws

What Kind of Man Are You

How To Have Success With God

# TAPE SERIES BY DR. KENNETH GILMORE

| | |
|---|---|
| New Covenant: Your Rights | 2 Tapes |
| What Is Biblical Faith? | 2 Tapes |
| How To Have Success With God | 5 Tapes |
| Money: God's Financial Plan | 2 Tapes |
| Unmasking Satanic Lies | 2 Tapes |
| The Authority of The Believer | 4 Tapes |
| The Power of The Tongue | 3 Tapes |
| God's Spiritual Laws | 6 Tapes |
| What Kind of Man Are You? | 3 Tapes |
| Principle Centered Living | 3 Tapes |
| The New Testament Church, Which One Is True? | 2 Tapes |
| The Battle For The Mind | 4 Tapes |
| Prayer | 4 Tapes |

# BECOME A COVENANT TRUTH PARTNER WITH KENNETH GILMORE MINISTRIES!

Because of the power that comes through fellowship, commitment and partnership, we invite you to join with Dr. Kenneth Gilmore in fulfilling the vision God has given him. Dr. Gilmore has been given a mandate to teach the Word of God in simple terms so that all can understand.

It's easy to become a Covenant Truth Partner. Simply fill out the form on page 101 and mail it to:

**Kenneth Gilmore Ministries**
**3615 SW 13th Street**
**Gainesville, FL 32641**

Our prayer for you is that as you enter covenant with us, God's blessings and manifold riches will be unleashed in your life.

Covenant Truth Partners have sought the Lord and received His confirmation of the worth of this ministry. Therefore, Partners are more than friends, they are loyal, trusted allies in the ministry. We value all of our Covenant Truth Partners and hold them up to God in prayer, minister to them with a personal monthly letter and offer from time to time discounted products for spiritual edification and growth.

**THERE IS VALUE IN COVENANT TRUTH PARTNERSHIP!**

*Yes. I'd like to become a Covenant Truth Partner in prayer and financial support with Kenneth Gilmore Ministries.*

---

Last Name

---

First Name                    Middle Initial

---

Street Address                Apartment #

---

City                          State    Zip

You can count on me for a monthly pledge of:

❑  $1,000          ❑  $500          ❑  $100

❑  $50             ❑  $25           ❑  $_____

❑  One time gift of $_____

# PERSONAL NOTES

www.ingramcontent.com/pod-product-compliance
Lightning Source LLC
Chambersburg PA
CBHW051839040426
42447CB00006B/612